DEATHS FOR THE LADIES

being

  a run
  of poems
    short poems
    very short poems
    and turns of prose

      entitled
        more formally

Deaths
for
the
Ladies

and
other
disasters

by

NORMAN MAILER

G. P. Putnam's Sons   New York

to Jean Campbell

DEATHS FOR THE LADIES

CHEERLEADERS

There is
no rest
for the wicked
wrote
Mr. M.
discovering
the art
of
the
short hair.

Explanations

The art of
  the
  short hair
  is that
  it
  don't
  go on
  for
  too long.

Cafe Society

It always
ruins
a
meal
to walk
half a block.

Amour

I still
love
him
deeply
   she said
   deeply
   out of her
   double
   chin.

Cheerleader

She
went to
Southern
Baptist
U
but
somehow
she nev-
er did
find out
who
John
the Bap-
tist
was.

Testaments

I never
   scored
   said
   snake.
It was
   Adam
   I wanted
    but
   Eve bought
   the cake.

Girl,
if you
was
a boy
and I
was
queer
I could
go
for
you

Oh God
I mustn't laugh
   said
   the evil old crow,
      it gives
      me
      crow's feet.

This is
genteel
poetry.
One thought
at a time.

what's doing
       mother

     well
I'll tell you
       brother
          you're
       the only
       brother
          I know
       who's got a
          mother
       that's your
          brother

Rip
the
prisons
 open.
 Put
 the
 convicts
 on
 television.

Illuminations

why do
  you
  always
  have
    to
    go off
    on a
      tangent
    said his mother.
why can't you
      be
      nice
      and
      clean?
Look!
      Your handkerchief
        has a hole in it.
      Let me give you a
        new one.

Don't you dare.
This way
  I can
  blow my nose
  and see what's
  going on
      said Rimbaud
      at six.

ROMANCE

Yin and Yang

It takes
eight
mild pleasures
to make one
small
mood
he said.

Oh, good,
said she,
you're in
an Oriental
turn
of
mind.
So
   let's go
to a
Chinese
   restaurant.

Pig-Pig

I'd rather
     be
psycho
     and
     savage
than
     sane
     and
         sour
     said
     the
     barbecued pork.

Gourmandise

1.

The wine
   was
   Sierra Blanca
   a California
      Sauterne.
But it had
   a moldy
   label
and a green
   rusted cork,
age and
   color
   of
   cobweb.
So we
   chose it
over a
   fine dry
   fast
   cool
   professional
   blond
      from
   Bordeaux.

2.

Yet when
      the
      nectar
         crested
         over
         the eddies
         of fume
         which rose
         from
      the dust
         of the cork,
         the wine
      was sour
         and
         squalid
            like
         bad breath
      on a good goose
         with bad teeth.
      Oh well,
         we murmured,
         never fall
            for a
            pretty face
               again.

You Chinese lady
I
Jahpanese
        gentleman
    that is
        vuhry
        rahr.

I must
admire
your
sense
of time

I was
about
to say
you
are
charming
and
you
said
yes,
of course.

The English
have a sense
of ambush
of vulgarity;
it is:
do you
descend
the steps
properly?

I'm not altogether
   nervous
I mean if we
   have another
   drink
   I think
      I could concentrate
         on the drink
         and not
            the
            time.

You're not as brave
          as your qualities
          he declared
So people like me
          say people like you
          and wonder if it
                    is true

Shadow of tears
          said she
Nothing to do with me

Night Clubs

Evil
  fingers
up
  and
  down
    my
  spine
    remind
          me
          that
          sex
          is
          not
          always
          divine.
          But
              sometimes
              it is
              with
              the most
              astonishing
              collection
              of
              horrible
              pig people.

In the Hallway

1.

My God,
        she said
I came
        in my
        hat

    This time
        baby
    take your
            shoes off
                he said

One
of the
things
I loathe
about
polite
society
is that
one
cannot
discuss
the nuances
of cannibalism.

2.

My God,
     he said
     this time
I came
     in *my*
     hat

     well,
take it
     off
       she said
I want
     to see
the ba-
     by
and how
     his hair
     will be.

Elegance

You
　have
one
of
the
　greatest asses
　　in
　　town
　　he said,

　　Is
　　it
extraordinary
　she
　asked?

No.　It's excellent. Please do
　　　　　　　　　　　stop

Eating in the Kitchen

Do you have
    a comb?

Use your
    fingers.

Transcendentalism

Talking
   of coming
      she said
   you make
      me
      feel
   furious
   and stupid.

You are
stupid
you're frightfully
   stupid
but I like
   the way
   you put
your freight cars
      together.

Repetition
kills the
hole
for its offers
dull the
soul

Explanations

The art of
  the
  short hair
  is that
  it
  don't
  go on
  for
  too long.

—my youth, that is to say, his promise
    has died
        said the swain
        as he said
    goodbye, and
            you
            are too
                lovely
                to
            some things
            are best
            left
            unsaid

Don't
fill
pauses,
you're
no
dentist.

Sayonara

Midnight
    said
    the
    lipstick
your mascara
    is mud.

        I know
            said the
            eyes
        but he was
            so
            attractive
        and he
        ended
        in the vast
            middle.

                Upper Middle
                    said the
                    ego
                    he kissed
                    my kooze.

                        'Twas booze
                            said Dame,
                            her nose
                            on
                                Fortune.

FAMILY

Orthodoxies

Jews
  who
  go to
  no
  synagogue
  have
  faces
   which
   change
  all
   the time.

Mon dieu,
Feinspan,
do I have
   to keep
   saying
   I'm pleased
   to be here
   Yes
I'm happy
   to be
   with those
   I love.
   Send the bill.

Unhappy Marriage

She says
    these things

I drop
    like dead
    meat-balls.

Cancer Gulch

What's
  he got?

  (Made
  a little
  money
Lost
  a little
  love)

Miami.

Circumcision

They say
   that
   women
   don't get
   cancer
   of the
   cervix
   as much
   from Jewish
     men.

They don't.

They give
   it
   to
   Jewish
     men.

In the first week
of their life
male jews
are crucified

Mon dieu, Feinspan,
in terror, I
exclaimed

the worst to be said
about mothers
is that they
are prone

to give

kisses

of con-
grat-
u-
lation

which make you feel
like a battleship
on which someone
is breaking
a bottle

Definition of a Hero:

He
  thrives
  in
  dikes.

Still . . .

        Mr
        Cancer
           and
           Miss
Catatonia
were
good
for each other

Mr
Cancer
    and
      Miss
Catatonia
were
very
good
for each other

but they were
        cousins
      so they
           did

  nothing
  about
  it.

You have
so many
poems
about
cancer.

It's me
or
my readers.

        If
Harry Golden
is the gentile's
Jew
        can I be-
come the Golden
Goy?

Don't
embroider
the angels
you strong
   Jew
or the
Hebrews
will say
   you're
American
you Nazi

MARRIAGE

What's authority
depriving you
of, Mr M?

Depravity.

The music of
    one's enemy
    gives life
if one is
    bold enough
    to savor
    his bride.
      Pride,
      the alternative
        is to suffer
        a wife.

Husbands

I want to
be a
fine
woman
and a
great
mother
to my
children
and
oh yes
you
she said

Wanted
without
wings
is stone
  dew
  lady

        You can't
        have
        a beer
        Momma
Gray   says
  mandarins no
  without
  grace
    is
    day   By God
    with prey if had a
    you're momma
    a king like
    with you
    feet I'd
    of clay never
        a
        reached
        the age
        of six

  No,
  lass
  I'm
  a
  mandarin
    said
    and reached   Wanted
    for a   without
    beer   wings
    first   is
    of the   stone
    blow   do

RAINY AFTERNOON WITH THE WIFE

Gray
without
grace,
day.

Gray
without
grace,
day.

Gray
without
grace

It takes a saint
    to stand up straight
at a time like this
    said the man
        on the bongo board

You're drunk
    said wife
If you fall down
    you'll break your
        nose again
    and let me tell you,
        pal,
    they don't paint their
        saints
    with broken nose
        these days
    Elegance is how
        the cookie
        cracks,
        you
        crumble

Repetition
  kills the
  soul
for its offers
  dull the
  hole
and sew
the wound
  of memory
  with death
  where life
      was once
      a tree
      nestling the root
      with gyres
       of sky
      and
        midnight's
        murmuring
         summer.

So long
  as
  you
  use
  a knife,
there's
  some
  love
   left.

the memory of
champagne I never drank
and kings I
    never kissed

Why do you still put on that face
powder which smells like Paris when
I was kicking seconal

do you
  descend
  the steps
    properly?

prac
tising
karate jabs
  to
 leather
 of booth,
      judo
      chops
        on
        edge
        of
        table.

why,
    asked
    young
    intent
    cowardly
    director
     know
     in
     theatre,

Why do that,
  why
  not leave
    violence
    alone?

Because
    said
      when learn
      do this

     can
     give
        penknife
      away

So long
  as
  you
  use
  a knife,
there's
  some
  love
   left.

  Murder

yoghurt
  fart
  church
  for
  art   blood
                and
                wood
                is
                bread
                            mother
                            menstrual
                            spike
                                and
                            mass
                                            foetus
                                            feathers
                                            food

                                    earning
                                    butter
                                    bone
                                    and
                                    break
                        fairies
                        father
                        flutes

        homocide is hairy

                                    morons murder mutes

            Royal
            is
            the
            rat who runs the race

The murderer
        said:

I owe
a death
to eternity

My soul
 is not
 complete
 until
 the eye
 of my
  vision
   is
         blinded
        by
      blood.

O sweet tear
    of the victim
    blind am I
    with love
      for thee.

You let everything stand
until it's knocked over
and then
you go over
and write
your own
ruins

Look, she said,
   he carried
   her across
   the street and
   over the slush
why don't you
   carry me?

Because you
   got the curse
   I got worse
   we been married
      ten years
   and when you're
   drunk you say
      anything.

Whatever
      you say, dear Romeo
      said
      Juliet
      carrying
         me
      across the street.

Your curse
I mean
your flow
don't
smell
too bad
said
candor
tipping
a lance
to tenderness

the nuance
    of being
    is to
    capture
    the
    seed

why
why daddy
    why is the sky blue?

child
  one would have
   to embrace
    your formal
        Why
        with coronations
        of intelligence
        purer than
        the purest
        reason
            of my
            heart

Beard is blonde
  it makes you
  drunk
  like that
  mommie-dolly,
     Daddy.

Gin is not water
  but she is white
  She makes
  you very
     drunk
  like mommie-daddy-dollie
       used to be
       when she-he
         fall
       boom-boom,
       off the wagon
       baby

The Good Lors

The Good Lors
    gave me
    my
    pretty
    face
The Good Lors
    is full
    of air
like a polar bear
    with
    lollypop
    breeze,
    daddy.

Love was here
today
and left us dry
did we deserve
Him?

doing the limbo bit
doing the limbo bit
it's good enough
for me

Punch up
  and counter
    by two's
      said the
      boxer
      who was dead
         half-dead
      for he knew
      the combo
        was three

Like we
  he deigned
  to waltz
He spewed up
  his salts
  like we.
God
  give us life
    by three
He won't.
He's dead
  from knuckle
    to knee
We killed Him
Thee and me
  tender lovers
  missing three
Too late
  a daughter
Never a son
The moon
  is begotten
but the lies
  not done
we were less
  than God
So he dared
  us all
Now the world
  will die
  for lack
  of a ball.

The Time Is Two, Not Three

I have this
    terrible
    image
    of you
    as the
        innocent
        agent of every
        provocateur
    said the prose
        of love
    determined
        to state
        a fact
        before
        the Fall

What a
    Summer
    we could
    have had
    if not
    for all that prose.

MODES

As it grows
   the flower
   breaks
   through the stone.

It has yet
   to prove
   itself
   against
   the clay.

Gray without grace
   day.

Art
cannot
recover
what was lost
to the cowardice
of the
knife
and yet
the blade
was invented
by a knight
in God's
employ
said Lear
mad with the
treacheries
of progress
and good
intention.

                    those
who are alive
look to others
for a mirror

the dead grow walls
half-dead, one drinks
            alone at night
            and writes poems

bad ones said self
sorry pity
should write so sad
and beg for tears

Poems
   written by
   masochists
    flop like cows
     in the meadow.
      Take pity on me
      they cry, pay
      attention, I
      am so sensitive
      to nature and
      full of milk

Poems
   should be like pins
   which prick the skin
        of boredom
        and leave
        a glow
      equal in its pride
      to the gait
      of the sadist
        who stuck
        the pin
        and walked away

"Our concern was speech, and speech impelled us
To purify the dialect of the tribe
And urge the mind to aftersight and foresight."

aftersight and foresight
the sound is dull
   in the ear
   like a bruise
   on fruit
   or the passage
   of bland taint
   in strong
   meat
So curious a man
   this Eliot
exquisite, forceful, superb
but dimmed in his climax
No wonder he caught
the spirit of an age

aftersight and foresight
   hole upon hole
   is the dead
   of poetry
   as a scheme in rhyme

A writer who
has power
should use it
to extract
such benefits
from his
publisher

as
give
his
words

room

to

breathe

I want my
line to
strike
like
a snake

A snake
can't strike
in a box

you break
up your
　　line
　　like
　　　ee
　　　cum
　　　　mings
　　I notice

　　　　n
　o　　heb　　　re　　a
ksitu　　　　pd
　　　　　iffe
　　　　　r
　　　　　e
　　　　　nt

I am looking
　for the
　fish who
　swim in the
　　　spaces

ee likes the
　　　herbs
　　　in the
　　　letters

　　　　　　　　　　　　　　　　r)

　　　　　　　　　　　　　ette

　　　　　besi desh e'sb

I have a simple mind
    and write my words
    to sweep across
    a broad cloth.
Rich talents go often
    to misers who make
    diadems of chocolate.
        the emperor is the
        emperor of ice cream
Excellent.

But the rich speak only
    to the purls of their lace.
    I want the whole wipe
    of the cloth
    even if I lose
    the rose,
    the sweetmeat
    and the throne
    of the moment.

Or do I delude myself
    and merely spit like
    a hoodlum
    into the wake of phaetons
    which drive away?

Some poems
   are mild
   and pleasant
   little children
      who bear no title
         and need none
      one doesn't notice
         their
         nakedness

A title
   is not
   a hat
   but
   a suit
      so
   sometimes
      I leave
   it at the
      bottom of
      the page,
      for
   I don't want
      all these poems
            to be
            naked.
            Some should be
                  standing
               with
               their trousers
               dropped to
                  their shoes.

Of course
   by this logic
   a title at the head
   is like a dress
   lifted over the breast

Prose
can pass
    into
poetry
when
    its heart
    is intense
For one
    can then
    dispense
    with whence
       went
       the verse.

Rhythm
  and rhyme
  may mask
    the movements
      of Time.
      Remember
    that the sound
    of Time
  is flesh.

Procurement

Lie down with dogs
   you rise with
                figs
   said the lady
   who was the loveliest
      of all my pigs.

Call this poem
   the Market Place
      cried
      the red-hair
            Negress
      who ball my ace.

Whores,
   I prate,
   make no ditties
      of my sores,
   for a pimp
      who shows no limp
      in the gait
            of his will
      has escaped
            all ill.

A MONOTONY
OF
ILLS

That ill
  whose
first
symptom
  is
  a
  monotony
    of nights

She believed
in the
efficacy
of patterns
So she worked
on the
Avenue
of the
Madison
and
sold
glop

The steel
and
glass
of some womb
which
lacked
the love
to
give me eyes

United Citizen's Protest

Gather
  me
  a
  monotony
  of
  names.

Cancer
is growing
ivy
professor
which   spreads
like college

A Well-Integrated Ego

People
   who
 despise
 themselves
   wear
   dingy
   under-
   garments
       said
       the
       psychiatrist
 flinging
the sorrows
   of his
   seed
       out, off, and away
           into a
           white
           linen
           hand-
           kerchief
           with a
           hand-
           rolled
           edge.

The Suburban Arts

Putting up
 with
 something
 you don't
         like
 and calling
 it charming
 spells
   age-in-the-face,
   dear,
   said
   the
   skin
   graft
 as it
 said
 hello
 and moved into its new home
                    on the neck

Charm

Drinker
with a
problem said:
I'll drink
to that
even if
it's not
quite
true.

A PAPER ON THE DIFFERENTIALS OF STATUS IN THE EGO-FORMATION OF THE JEWISH HOMOSEXUAL

One
  of
  the bones
of
contention
  is
  that
  Franz
calls
me
a rabbi
and
I
call
him
one

Chinese Meeting

Let us go
    our
    separate
        ways
        and
    meet again
     said I
     to the
     diseases.

     Don't leave
     was told
     me.
You director
    of corporation.

Togetherness

My flesh must smell like an old tire
my sex is bitter and gone
my days are leafless and all sleep
    said the housewife
    going to the specialist
one knows what kind

but in the waiting room
she was racked by a plague
from the pots of the American
      miasma—our magazines,
     and so lady murmured
         too quietly
even for her mind to hear:

Reader's Digest, please save *your* soul
and leave mine free to contemplate
eternity which must be more
    than I glimpse for myself now
    an endless promenade
across a field of baked old beans
    a cataract of dishwater
    regurgitated by the memory
of champagne I never drank
    and kings I never kissed

A wandering in prose:

for Hemingway

November, 1960

That first unmanageable cell
of the cancer which was to
stifle his existence arrived
to him on a morning when by
an extreme act of the will
he chose not to strike his
mother. Since this was
thirtysix hours after he
had stabbed his wife, and
his mother had come at a time
when he wished to see no one
in order to savor the woes
and pawed prides of his soul,
(what a need for leisure
has the criminal heart) his
renunciation of violence
was civilized, too civilized
for his cells which proceeded
to revolt. But then it is
the thesis of this summary
that civilization spawns
cancer in every corner of
every church whose smell
is stale with the fatigues
of such devotion as lost its
memory on the long road
to ecstasy from
habit.

Witchcraft

When I was
   your age
   twenty
     seven
a dame
    could
    say
I'll put
   a curse
   on
     you.

On
    I would say
    put a curse
      on me
   and wonder
     why
     my voice
     would break.

One
nerve
screams
before
you
fall
said
the
ledge
on
the
window
in
the
nineteenth
floor

WITCHCRAFT

You've got
the
smell
of the
corporation
again
said the lover
to his lady

No, said she,
I've
been
to
  my
hairdresser

I won't stay in
    with married men
    any more
    said the wise girl
        they're too agreeable,
        it's a little too much
            like curling
            up ·
        with the good book.

You mean
        a
        good book

Oh, dear,
        did I say
        the
        good book
        sighed the witch.

Vodka is fine
we agreed,
one can keep
one's character,
it doesn't do
funny things
to the style
of the soul
departing,
it doesn't
get into
the end
of one's
fingers
and leave them weak.

You must never let
anything
get into
the end
of your fingers
but
     Love
said evil
getting up
to get another drink.

The call girl
  walked along
  the bar
  escorted by
   a plump
      virile
      pomaded
      hip businessman,
      minor league Mafia,
  and behind them
      trailed a smell
        of stale
        sulphur.

   O sex
      you are dying
      I know
      but in
         whose name?
         and for what
                cause?

Do your duty
    said I
    to the beauty
  as she turned
    from love
    (the act)
    and sauntered
        down the
        hall
        to
        commune
        with porcelain,
        fluorescent light
    and hound's sigh
        of lavatory water
        languishing
            after the
            souls
        my beauty
            chose
            to taste
            and flush
                away.

(Never
grieve
the
death
of
little
fish)

I know
a town
with
sighs
of
sea
smiled
the
white
witch

dreamed,
  said the cavalier
  to the lady,
that I gave myself.
Was it poison
or nectar?

Who can remember
  said the tear.

I can
  said the child,
and fuck you.

not you
but your cure
do I fear
O my love
for your cure
is a
      curse
upon me

Somehow
I've never
quite
believed
in women
   said the Lord
as he gave
a sad
goose
to Adam
and banished
him.

CANNIBALS

Screenwriters

The Devil is a mirror
  but a true lover
  is God's mirror
        said
        William Blake
        on a bad day.

Turn over in your grave
        Bill
            said I
        make way for the wild
        and young.

Cannibals
   are
   the
     mirror
     of
     the
     scene.

Southern Queens

I've always been
    ass-deep
    in men
    King-size
    said the Protestant
    lady-stenographer
    to the Southern
    professional
    football player

I wish you'd
        take
        your big
                toe
                off
        this rocking
                chair,
        King-Size,
        you're
                making
                me
                dizzy.

Cold War

The Lady
    was
    quite
    a queen
        in her
        own right
    but she said:

You're a great man
    you're a
        very
        great
        man
    only please
        why can't
        you be
    considerate
        of others
        as well?

Heh heh,
    can't do two things
        at once
        said Rasputin.

Burnt Umber
        Yellow Ochre

A crap,
    said
    the
    pedant
    picking
        his
        paws
    is an
    idealist
    who has
    not yet decided
        he is worthy
        to be considered
            a shit.

Mon dieu, Feinspan,
in terror, I
    exclaimed
abjure the
Anglicans

Freud's Folly

I know
a guy
who
used
to come
in
his socks
and throw
them up
on top
of his
closet
said the girl
  He was
an actor
  He
wanted
to play
King Lear

I wasn't
supportive
to him
  I mean
like
he would
fantasize
about
suicide
pacts
with me.

Let's
stamp out
bad dialogue.

That's *your* problem
said the
toad.

Jazz is
  new art
with great soul
      say
  new com
    missar
    Ivan
    Tcherkoff
    Djugo

    Russia
    that is
    union
    full
    people's
    opinion
    approve
    bing and
    bang
        with bong
    of black
    man boogie.

Crazy
    said
    the vein

  Now that fuzz is flying

Jacks and Jills

In my line
    of work
    you meet
some of
    the
    nicest
    people
        said
    the going
        young
        mortician
    Many of them
        are waiting
        for the wills
        to come through
    Sometimes
        there are
        chills
        or spills.
    Ills alert me.
    My name is
        Vowel Chimes, Esquire

Registers

You must meet her.
She's rather nice.
  she's an
    absolute
    brigand
    who came out
    of a whorehouse
      in Baltimore.
Then she married
    a Jewish man
    from Macy's
And then my father.
Now she has
    the most terrible
    dining room
    in New York.
It's all gold.
Last year
    she finished
    decorating her house
    and charged
    one hundred dollars
    a plate
    to let people in.
No drinks.
  Of course
    it was for
    a marvelous charity
      called Baskets.
    For people
      without
      arms
      or legs.
Isn't that nice?

I
  was
  hysterical
  stated
  the girl
      I
dropped
my
  god
damned con
tact lens
     down
     the drain

Then
this
creep
called
at four
  A.M.

                   Hel
                     lo Kook
                     he said

                 Guess what:

                     I just
                     found
                     your
                     contact
                       lens.

The Adventurer

I don't mind
   a party that
        gets
   a little rough
but did you
   have to throw
        up
        in my foyer
        said the lady.

Despair never   Ladies
   said the   teach
   drunk,   one
I'll pick   lecon
        it up   seul
   I'll really   one
        pick it up   that
        because I don't   the
        believe   essence
        in leaving   of
        my leavings   perfume
        at a ladies'   is
            door   duty
        when she's a lady
           like you
           you crappy
           old
           unhappy
            bag of an armpit
            anyone ever
            say
            you're beautiful
            said the drunk as he fell on his nose
            trying to kiss lady and her fortune.

How can you
    say
you're
only
three-quarters
        a man,
why you're
        completely
        a man
        said the
            lady
            in a
            three-quarter voice.

Definition of a Lady

She grasps
the root
while kissing
the bud

something
about
the
smell
of a cop
when he's
groping
you

It's excellent. Please do
stop

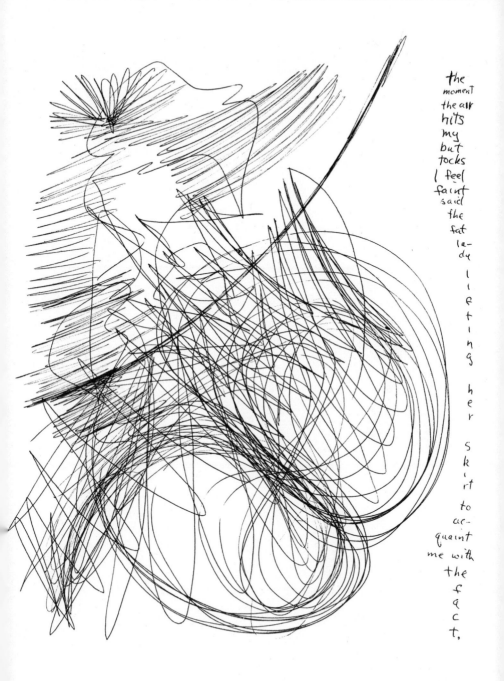

the
moment
the air
hits
my
but
tocks
I feel
faint
said
the
fat
la-
dy
lif-
t
i
n
g
her
s
k
i
r
t
to
ac-
quaint
me with
the
f
a
c
t.

DEVILS

One of us
will
be
better
looking
when it's
all
over.

Babes,
you got
    nostrils
    like
  devil's feet

Courtship

It's a fine wine
    hearty as one drinks it,
                    peppery
            yet it seems
                to come
                florid
                and
                soft

Yes, I answered,
    we have an
    old peasant
    saying:
It's a fine wine
                but the devil
                farted
                in it
                once.

"The worst to be said about mothers
is that they are prone
to give kisses of congratulations
which make you feel
like a battleship
on which someone
is breaking a bottle"
said the figure of speech
in a voice
which
awarded art
to itself.
Metaphors may be heartless.
In the salon they are savage.
One enters rooms wet
with a razor's light
from the tongue of
fifteen bloods
ready to dissect
the fornications
of their fathers.

Their hope?
That
surgical excisions
upon the past
may illumine
the flesh of the
company
with a luminous blaze
pure as wit
in a moment of murder.
Not all light is love.

Hymns

The sweetest
        song
I ever heard
        was
    the sound
    of each
            tongue
            on the
    other's
            bung
    said a choirmaster
        for the Devil.

Mr Answer Man
     how many lives
     has a cat?

As many
     as the
     mood
     he uses
     up

Mood
is
a
congregation
of souls
in the cells

I know
   the
   belly
   of Mexico
   must smell
   like the trail
         of a
         woodburning
                  bus.
Oh Mexico
   if all your
            sewers
            were scents,
            and your
            modern
            apartments
            lost their cracks
      would your women
            cease to look
                  so sad
      and your men so silly
Oh Mexico
   let your deserts
                  bloom
      and your mustaches
            turn to gold.

The Economy of Love

Your eyes
        are beautiful
    said my
        love.
Yes said I
            eyes of
            mine have
                seen your
                breast
                and so are
                    beautiful.

    (but my heart
            was immersed
            in that
            calculus
            of the soul
            which measures
                the profit
                and cost
            of conversions
                from beauty
                to power)

Your eyes
            are beautiful
            said my love
            and have
                left
                me.

I never
scored
said
Snake

A *wandering in prose: for* Hemingway
Summer, 1956

Why do you still put on that face
powder which smells like Paris when
I was kicking seconal and used to
get up at four in the morning and
walk the streets into the long wait
for dawn (like an exhausted husband
pacing the room where you wait for
the hospital to inform you of wife
and birth) visions of my death seated
already in the nauseas of my tense
frightened liver—such a poor death,
wet with timidity, ordure and the
muck of a Paris dawn, the city more
beautiful than it had ever been, warm
in June and me at five in an Algerian
bar watching the workers take a
swallow of wine for breakfast, the
city tender in its light even to me
and I sicker than I've ever been,
weak with loathing at all I had not done,
and all I was learning of all I would

now never do, and I would come back
after combing the vistas of the Seine
for glints of light to bank in the
corroded vaults of my ambitious and
yellow jaundiced soul and there back
in bed, nada, you lying in bed in hate
of me, the waves of unspoken flesh
radiating detestation into me because
I have been brave a little but not nearly
brave enough for you, greedy bitch,
Spanish lady, with your murderous
Indian blood and your crazy purity
hung on courage in men as if it were
your queen's own royal balls, and I
would lie down next to you, that smell
of unguent and face powder bleak and
chic as if the life of your skin depended
now not on the life my hands could give
in a pass upon your cheek, but upon the
arts of the corporation mixing your
elixirs in hundred gallon vats by
temperatures calibrated to the thermostat,
bleak and chic like the Hotel Palais
Royale ("my home away from home" we had
seen written by Capote in his cuneiform
script when the guest book was passed
to me for the equivocal cachet of my
signature so dim in its fashion that
year) and I took up the pen thinking
of the buff-colored damp of our indif-
ferent room where we slept in misery
wondering if we had lost the loots of
anticipation we had commanded once so

fierce in one another—or was it only
me? for that is the thought of a lover
when his death comes over him in that
scent of the creams you rubbed on your
face while I slept the half-sleep of
the addict kicking the authority of
his poison—how bitter and clean was
the taste of the seconal. And now in
March of sixty-one the scent of that
cream came over me again as you kissed
me here at this instant, wearing it
again, knowing I detest it because again
it drives the secret of my poor augure
for eternity into those caverns of my
nose which lead back among the stalactites
of the nostril to the dream and one's
nightly dialogue with the fine verdicts
of the city asleep, and all souls on the
prowl talking to one another in the
dark markets of heaven about the future
of what we are to be if one obeys the
shape we gamblers have given to that
tool of destiny—our character. And the
smell of the corporation is still on
your skin mocking what I have done to
mine.

DEATHS

Mr. Answer Man
     define
       a
          junkie.

Soul
    without
    a world.

Nothing
     or
     nausea
     is the choice
     for those
        who
        lose.

one
nerve
screams
before
you
fall
said
the
ledge
on the
window
in the
nine-
teenth
floor

the remembered musk
of wood-smoke at dusk
in Cambridge
            and New Haven

One
nerve
screams
before
you
fall

Let
at least
a drink
be
named
after me
said the poet
sealing his
fate
for
no bar
in the land
would tease
the police.

I find
  that
  most
  of the people I
        know
    are immature
    and cannot
        cope
        with reality
    said the suicide
His death
  followed
    a slash on each wrist.
Fit
was this end
for blood
  in its flow
  reveals
what a furnace
  had burned
    in the dungeon
    of his unconscious

Burn and bleed

He coped with
  reality
  too well.

It was unreality
    which waited
    on a midnight trail
      in that fierce
        jungle of eternity
        he heard murmuring
      on the other side

Oh, night of the jungle,
    God of mercy
    wept the suicide
    do not ask me
    to reconnoiter
      this
        dark
        trail
      when I am now
        without
        hands.

Hunting

men who go out to kill deer
   hope to find in the blood
   of the new dead
the poems of my flesh
   said the deer in the forest

Koan

Master
is
beauty
something
which
changes
you
into
something
which
can change?

There's one thing about you,
baby
    said Sir Cirrhosis,
of all the witches I've known
you're the merriest
    and he died
        with style.

He died with style
    said the witch.

Yes,
    said the wind
    which rose from the spirit
    of the gin
give him honor in Hell.

He played
a
lonely
figure
on a
muted
harp.
It was
a sweet
sad
little
lay.

Royal
is
the
rat who runs the race

doing the limbo bit
doing the limbo bit
          it's good enough
                    for me

Gray without grace
day.

I know
a town
with
sighs
of
sea
smiled
the
white
witch

I know
a town
which
sails
the
sun

I know
a town
where
light
is dry
and
boats
come
home
with
silver
in their
hold

THE HARBORS
OF THE
MOON

where
boats
come
home
with
silver
in their
hold

(Do not
grieve
the
death
of
little
fish
They
are
lights
which
smell
the
deep)

I know
a town
with
sighs
of sea

white
with
the
tides
of me

white
as the
spine
of the
sea.

It would
be
an aid
if the
blind
came
to the
game
because
their ears
are
clean
said
the dream

Death in the Mountains

We rented three horses
    in San Miguel Allende.
Two were to be tame.
But indeed the groom
    brought only two
            to the door.
Oh, Senor, said he,
    the third horse
            has a cold.

On the next day
    there were still but two
Relámpago and Gavilan.
We rode those horses—
    they were devils.
In three days
    they threw me
            three times.

It was only on the night
            of our departure
    that we learned
    our horses
    were mad.

Oh, Senor, said the groom
    the third horse has a cold.

by the third day
He
said
You know
of course
that I was
sentenced
to be
Your son
because
I cannot
bear pain

MOODS FOR SUNDAY

America should have
two churches
one for people
who smoke
and one for those
who don't

The
  cigarette
  smoker
  said

  I'd
  rather
  waste it
  than give
  it

  away

why hast Thou
        forsaken me
        said the brave boy
    didst make
    a pact
    to smoke
        cigars
        with the snake,
        while
        I
        was
        here?

                    I
love Christ
said the Epis
copalian school
instructor
                    but
he's not
in the most
secure of taste

because
none of us
                    are
altogether
at ease
                    here
in the light
of the green
        cut
    out of the
            wood

for in the light of the wood
green from the cut, we killed Him
thee and me

Crossing

The Lobby

of the

Taft

That's
the
best
thing
he
ever
did
to run the money-changers out of
the
temple,
that's
the
best
thing
he
ever
did
said
the
hat
from
Ind-
iana

Certain Evictions

In the first week
        of their life
        male jews
        are crucified
The pain
        is
        exquisite

To discover
        the tip
        of your future
    by losing it
        is a fair
        price
        to pay
            for having been
        once so tense
        as to fail
        the race
        when
        He
        chose
        a Jew
        without a future
            to save it.

Grace.
    In the first week
        of their life
        grace is crucified.

The Corners
of a
Square

1.

It would
be
an aid
if the
blind
came
to the
game
because
their ears
are
clean
said
the dream.

2.

I would
be
afraid
of those
who
hear and
do not
see
said
the word.

3.

I am
in
love with
those who
come
with their
wound to
me
said the
mood
for
those who
see
and do
not hear
wound
others
with their
voice.

4.

Those who
hear
and do
not see
give
alms
to Eve
and
other
ill
said
the peace
which comes
from
the police.

Colored people
   have beautiful
   hands
   said
   the pause.

                              Listen
                                 mother
                                 fucker
                                    said
                                    the mood
                              Stop quoting me.

Mood
 is a
congregation
of souls
     in the cells.

Those
 who govern
 a body
 of murdered hopes
  and
  cold will
 are subject to
  sudden defeats
   of mood
   so severe
  as to pose
   the question:

Is mood a temple
 which gives us
 sanctuary
 against
  the desire
  of our cells
 to return to
   their beginnings
  under a
  new master
  who promises
  that he
  will not
  repeat
 the hesitations,
 compassions
     and
 aesthetic
     com-
 punctions of God
  about
   pleasure
   profit
  and
   progress
 but
  instead
   will rip up
   the roots
and give us
the broad
macadam
     of
civic virtue
tranquilized pain
eternity
     without fire
and sucaryl
for the syrup
   of the peach.

To the lower classes

Noblesse
    Oblige
  has one rule
      and
  one rule only

You must be
    so nice
    so bright
    so quick and
    so well turned
        that
    no one need
        tell you
        a second time.

Tell me what?
    that the world
        is well-lost
        for love
    and the upper
        classes
        are the
        law above?

I tell you this:
    if the
    upper classes
    are kin to God
        in style—
    (which is one hypothesis
        we do not ignore:
            how else account
            for elegance?)

if the
upper classes
are kin to God
    in style
then God has no love
but guilt, nor a style
apart from fashion,
no courage but to
do in duty
            what
one does not desire
and no worth
but for His love
            at beauty
For there
        is noble's work
their plea:
            that they
love in truth
with all sense
        of Christian
        love
    divorced from self
    the air of beauty
        and her pomp.

The poor know naught
        but death
    they do not free
    they obliterate.

Stripped of its
       distinctions
life is a flat city
    whose isolated spurs
    cut the sky
    like housing projects.
Think of the air
    whose heart is bruised
    by touching such artifacts.
    (*Does* the cutworm forgive
                the plough?)

I tell you, say the rich,
       the poor are naught
       but dirty wind
       welling in air-shafts
       over the cinders
       and droppings of
       the past, their
       voices thick
       with grease
       and ordure,
       sewer-greed
       to corrode the ear
       with the horrors
       of the past
and the voids
       of new stupidity.
One could drown
       waiting for the poor
       to make
       one fine distinction.
Yes, destroy us
       say the rich
       and you lose
         the roots
         of God.

Destroy them
　　　say the poor
we cannot breathe
nor give
until we etch
　　　on their rich nerve
　　　the cruel razor
　　　and heartless club
　　　　　　of our past,
　　　those sediments of
　　　　　　waste
　　　　　　which curbed
　　　　　　　　our genes
　　　　　　　　and flattened
　　　　　　　　the vision we
　　　　　　　　would give
　　　　　　the chromosome.

Yes, destroy them
　　　say the poor
　　　burn them, rob them
　　　gorge their tears
and such half of beauty
　　　lost to pomp
　　　will flower
　　　unglimpsed wonders
　　　in the rose,
　　　will flower
　　　unglimpsed wonders
　　　in the rows.

I wonder,
　　　said the Lord
I wonder if I know the answer
　　　　　　any more.

sir
your
short
hairs
take
on
airs
said the
dowager

IN NEW YORK
IT'S NOT ENOUGH
TO BE POLITE

In New York
it's not
enough
to be polite,
one must
be
brutally polite,
to wit:
variations
observe
the theme
of foul
economy
Shithead
follows
up your
bunny
honey
in
balance
and pro-
priety
Jew
bastard
if said
in a
Village
bar
is as
gentle
as
spade
creep
Fuck off
can be

returned
with
three
stiff
fingers
to the
plexus
or the
neck
The
rule
is
keep
cool
This
is
New
York

Sex in the Mafia—
                    Weak Son Division

Darling
    said the lady
    being wooed
When I'm
    with
    you
I don't
    have
    the
    feeling
    you're
    ever
    sincere

Cheer up, pal,
    said the
    cigar,
    it's im-
    possible
    to do something
            good
    without
    being
        like
        halfass
        sincere,
Excuse my smoke.

Coffee

Panhandling
the Bowery
on Sunday aft
with gray sky
and no butts
we had an
argument
over the
      merits
of frozen food
versus canned.

Canned is awful,
I said, it comes
out half dead.

Yeah, said Red
      but
      frozen
      is stone.

Paddy Chayevsky Revisited

will you
    enjoy
    it
  said
    the
    virgin.

listen
    said
    the Bronx,

see your
    lawyer,
    draw
    up a
    contract
which
    stipulates
    I got
    to
    enjoy
    it,

and
    I'll
    still
enjoy
    it,
    golden
      girl.

Have you
ever
tasted
the peach
asked
the oracle?

Yes,
said the
money,
flesh and fuzz.

Killers

Don't
bug
me
or I'll
gas
you
said
the creep.

Kiss off,
    said gun,
    can't you
      see
      I'm
      here
to do a job on the soul across the
                        street?

Very hip guy
very hip
which is to
say
that he knows
a
little
about
fornication
and a lot
about
how
to
employ
its
teachings
in the
business
world.

I'm rich
   said
   Irish
      derby
      slopping
       a drink
       on the
       floor

So I've always
       missed
       the pleasures
       of the poor.

          Taste his spit!
             said the sawdust
             it's a scandal
          and a shame

       Naught but outer limbo
          said the roach
             on his way
             on his fraught-filled
                   way, on his fraught-
          filled way to the door
                and toward the
                      stair
                      of his own.

When he reached
        the cracked enamel
        in the kitchen
            of his pad
        he made a
            tour
        of quarters
            leaving
            molecules
            like pennies
            on the oilcloth
                of the
                poor—
        five molecules
                of scotch
                to every
                        plate

But the fumes had drunk
        his mind to stuff
        and roachie slept
        an emperor's sleep
    dreaming of previous lives
        in derby hats
    when he had slopped
            the whiskey
            to the floor
    crying for the pleasures
            of the poor.

I used
to think
my life
would be
a
destiny
and now
I realize
it's but a fate
said a man
I met
in Bellevue
for
stabbing
his
brother
with a
kitchen
knife

1.

Men
  who work
    at Time
  have a
    life expec-
    tancy
    which is
    not long
  said the
  young man
    from
  Newsweek

Junkies

2.

Those
  who
  bat out
  the poop
    for
the other sheet
    don't use up
    a thing
    in
    my scheme
    of space
  said the
  young blood
    from Yale

3.

But
in the
evenings
    they met
    and had
    beers
    together
    in Irish bars
    which looked
    the proper hair
        of fashion
        askew
        the type

And as they drank
        into
    the warm
    spring
    evenings
    the remembered musk
of wood-smoke at dusk
        brought
        tenderness
            to
        liberty
        and
        irony
            to
            fate
        and they
            would

chant
a song
in
bitter
prose which
        went:

                we
                are
                saving
                our
                pennies
            to buy
        a bond
        to aid
        the drive
        of the United
Junkies   Corporations of Community
        who wish
        to construct
        a new
        and im-
        proved
        rest home
        for all
        the
        cancer-
        pushers
        on the
            team.

    Boola-
        boola,
        boola-
            boole.   I've always
                                    missed
                                    the pleasures
                                    of the poor.

Harlem East

Now
  these
  children
  want me
  to roast
    their
     tea
  said The
  Man with
    the bag.

Do they
  think
  I'm a
  mother
  with
  shades
  and a
  furled
  umbrella?
  Go to sea,
    Jim,
  I have
    something
    in my
     head
    that
    would
    really
    kill
    you

LOVERS

She's a
   bitch
   said
   the witch
   in a tone
   which clarified
   the eternal meaning
   of the consonants.

Vowels,
    your honor,
    said the voice,
    there is no
        justice
    in human verdict.

                Justice

We were speaking
   of witches
   said
   the judge
      I prefer
      to ignore eternity
        and the color
        she gives to
        human voice.
        It is better
        to chase consonants
        than vowels.
    Consonants are
     fact and force
     clear as compound
          interest
   vowels are hot eyes
    in hard bodies
    bleeding for trouble.

Eternity is first heard
        on the pigeon's wing
        of a sigh
        replied the voice,
        breathing alas
        at all that passes
        and does not happen,
Judge, Your Honor,
        Bind me over
        to the next of size
        for I do dream
        that love there may be
           in human verdict.

Sex

Superhighways
cut through
profit and
passion
and so
inhabit
the moon
before we've
learned
its mountain
road
which
winds
in
slow
curves
of the
root
toward
the ore
and her nugget.

He pissed
  with
  a
  stern
  loneliness
  leaving
    a fierce
    and
    disgruntled
    smell
    of the past.
  His future
      was not
      so empty
        as he declared,
        a girl with
        music and grace
        ugly of face
        was waiting
          for him.

Hey—
    you
      sleep
      deep—
    but what a sight
      see
    you
        soon
        beautiful
        I hope

(Since the lady
        found this note
        by her telephone
        on awakening
        in an empty bed
        after a one-night
        stand, she called
        her best friend
        a girl, and said,
            Guess what?
            I feel like
                Earth
                Mother.)

Hey, you sleep deep
but what a sight.

Funky Love

We really ought, she said
to be able to stay together
  without making love
    all the time.

Yes, he said smugly
I'm sure it's my fault.

Yes, she said smugly
you smell so greedy
              and good

Swarms and swarms
  of love
    smug, smug, smug.

Lineage

She never blushed
    until
    she smelled
the fine cheat
    in
    the line
    of the succession
and then
    she flushed
    furiously
for she thought
    the smell
    adorable,
    it was
    so
    rich
    to rise
        from
        the poor.

You may not love me
          I said
     but I love you.
Well I love you,
          she said
          so
          bad luck.
We loved each other
          very much.
I do not think
we had taken
          a good wash
          in three weeks.
     It would have been
          the next wrong
          to murdering
               a child.
     What the hell
          we were both
          thirty
          forty
          tired, tried
          sad, foul
     We thought we
          had betrayed
          something
          forever,
And She forgave us.
Or thus we hoped.
          So, bad luck
          muttered the
               horror
               of old
               habit,
               I will die
               if I lose
               your love.

Mangled, morgued
birched and bruted
 they stepped forth
 death their suitor
  cursed by hair
  which knew no sea
 for they were hawks
  upon the mood
  of their
   own
   blessing.
Besides
 they still found
 other people attractive.

Slack were the yaws
 tight the jaws
 hurricane
 the air
  of waiting
  while they discovered
  less
  than they were offered.

Mangled, morgued
birched and bruted
 they scattered
  in their souls
 waiting
  for the
  curse.

Writing a poem together
  the lady, a poet, said:
       "scuffled"
I said: "scattered."
The word was a key
   to the lock
   in the soul of the poem.
 We fought
   and said goodbye.
   "Do not change my poem"
     was a switch
     to the execution
     of our little love
     for the evening, for
     words in the nerve
     of becoming
     are feathers
       of eternity
       (insofar
         as a poem may become
         the death of another
         who believed the poem
         and so ended in some alley
         of bad venture
         fighting for it)
Words are feathers
   tickling our choice
   into earth
   or sea, ocean
   or air,
       or that province
       of the hole
       inhabited by dialogues
       between God, Nothing, and the Devil.

Naked

Where
the act fails
sleep binds
the bodies
of those
who
were
born
to love
each
other
in
truth.

THE
INAUGURAL
BALL

antibiotics
psychoanalysis
research projects
vitamins
awards
crash programs
crash diets
symposiums
foundations
rest
rehabilitation
tranquilizers
aspirin
surgery
brainwashing
lobotomies
rises in status
box office boffo
perversions

                                    tenderness
                                         to
                                    liberty
                                    and
                                    irony
                                         to
                                         fate

O sex
 you are dying
 I know
 but in
    whose name?
    and for what
            cause?

we were less
  than God
So he dared
  us all
Now the world
  will die
  for lack
  of a ball.

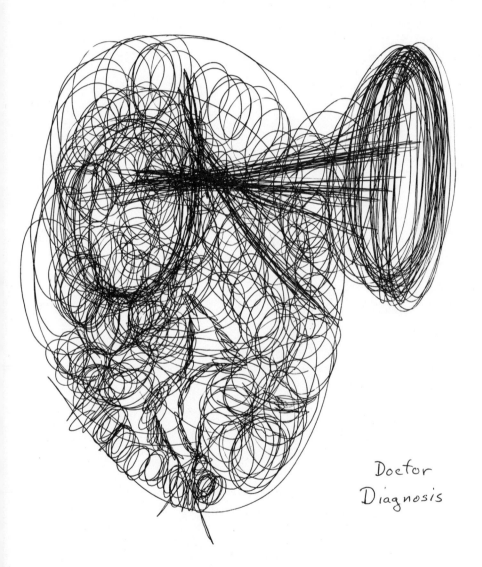

Doctor
Diagnosis

Men
who are not
    married
    and grow beards
    are insecure,
    said the CIA
before
    it went
    to Cuba.

Heroes

I applied
to
Harvard
but I've
picked
Yale
Columbia
and
Brown
as my
        fall-back
        said the
        child of
        the new
        frontier.

Sex in the High Schools

Johnny
 what
 can I do
 said the
 girl
I gotta pee

She was in a
 strange pad
 three hours long

Why just
 come here
 princess,
  said
  Johnny
 and I'll lead you
 to the throne
 who serves as sink.

Oh, indeed, Johnny
 said the girl
 you're funny.

Basketball
used to
be a game
for short
tough
squatty
little Jews
who were tough
as Italians.

Now it's church
for the tall jobs
said the handicapper's
decaying
tooth.

Logic

A. When Napoleon
        met Goethe
        it was the
        Emperor
        who wrote the poem.

B. When I met
        Kennedy . . .

C. Either:
                Jack
                is a
                greater
                    man than
                        me,
                Or—
                    times have
                        changed.

I hear
our
president
is quite a bounder
said a
would-be
thrush
of our
time

Mister
 Answer
  Man
  what do you think
  of the Chinese
  Communists?
      asked
      the poet
      (who
        thought
        of himself
        as a
        blade of g

                r

                a

                s

                s)

        A power
        lawn
        mower

A plague is
        coming
        named
            Virus Y S X
        still unsolved
        promises to be
                    proof
                    against
                    antibiotics
                    psychoanalysis
                    research projects
                    vitamins
                    awards
                    crash programs
                    crash diets
                    symposiums
                    foundations
                    rest
                    rehabilitation
                    tranquilizers
                    aspirin
                    surgery
                    brainwashing
                    lobotomies
                    rises in status
                    box office boffo
                    perversions
                        and
                        even
                        a
                        good
                        piece
                        of

When that unhappy day
        comes to America
        let the Russians
        take over.
The best defense is
                infection.

(*Penicillin, chief weapon against venereal disease, is losing some of its punch. In 1943, 100,000 units of the drug were considered sufficient to effect a cure for gonorrhea. Today, doses of one million units are commonplace, and many physicians inject more than two million. Yet in Japan, for example, 30 percent of gonorrhea cases have failed to respond even to massive doses.*—Reader's Digest, MARCH 1961)

One
man's
meat
is an-
other's
milk
said the aficionado

Interplanetary

    as
    he
    skimmed
       the
        cream
    from his
    third drop
    and transported it holy
          to a
          tube which knew a
          syringe.

Of course,
    Mr.
    President,
    replied the matador
    to the intercom,
        we
        are
        indeed hot
            on
            the track
            of the
            wonder
            disease

            and
            are
        now feeding
        the penicillin
        its dose.
    Expect to save
        it
        and all
        group-related
            compounds
            if the
        television
            does not collapse.

put down
   that
   penicillin
      dad

get me
a dose
of gonorrhee

              doing the limbo bit
              it's good enough
                    for me

Distinctions

I'd
  rather
  be
  Screwed-up
  than
  Sick

anyone ever
say
you're beautiful
said the drunk
as he fell
on his nose.

release
the anger
contained
in a fart

and there'll
be power
enough
to reach
the moan

said the
physicist
as he
assumed
the throne

I mean
the moon.

A Cure for Cancer

A
 cure
  for
   cancer
    is
    to
   visit
   the
  moon

A. A.

I think
I'll switch
 from ginger ale
    now
to a
nice
  glass
  of
  Soda

Catnip for the Kiddies

Does the football team
        eat a lot?
        asked the
        announcer

Oh, I think so, Jim
            those football
            boys are
            pretty big
            down there.

When did you two
            titans
            last meet?

Well, bud, it was in
            November
            1960
            that fateful
            gray day
            in Philadelphia
            The weather was
            so bad we almost
            stayed in our
            hotel and ate each other.
            Our boys were
            keyed-up, I tell you.

Every time
I move
I squash
    something
    said
    Loathesome.

rip the prisons
                open
        put the
                convicts
                on
                television

1.

I feel
 like
I've been
 through purga-
     tory, Catherine
           said.
     Sometimes
     I think
       it won't
         be bad
           when
           we die
           because
       we've served
         part
         of
         purgatory al-
             ready.

Yes.
 It's been
   bad.
   But
 twelve years
   ago
     we were
     good.

Oh, darling, good, she agreed,
                 so good.
     I used to think
         it would
         be
         endless,
         I
         thought
         it would
         be always,
         but it wasn't, it
             turned out
             to be
             such a little
             taste
             of
             heaven
             for twelve
             long years.

2.

A little taste
        of heaven
    is all we get,
        baby,
        said
        Caryl
        Chessman
        through the
        microphone
        and plate
            glass
            window
        of the visitor's
                room
            under
        the shotguns
        eyes
        bellies
        and blue serge suits
        of the guards
        who guard
    the sacred heart
    of the Republic.

Freedom of the Press

Let every
   writer
   tell his
         own
         lies
That's freedom
      of the
      press.

doing the limbo bit

it's good
   enough
   for
   me

To the ghost of his late highness the Senator

Another orphan
    said McCarthy
    let's have a high mass
    and kiss her ass
    before we kick
    her cunt in,
    sister superior.

Ooooooo
Is this poem good for the Jews?
    asked Reverend Godspee
    of the Inter-Faith Council
        for Tolerance
            Muscular Dystrophy
                and
            Communities-of-Cancer

Kick his cunt in too
            said McCarthy
Reverend Godspee is
            a Communist

You're fucking aye
        said all the louts
        in all the bars
        in Queens
      and they were right
        for once.

The Establishment

You
 can't
and
you
won't
print that,
    said
    the Goddess
        in a voice
        which
            released
            half
            her
            souls
    from prison
            and
            dropped
            them
            into
    Hell.

May I say
you're
the
first
bigot
I
ever
balled.

Or do I delude myself
and merely spit like
a hoodlum
into the wake of phaetons
which drive away?

At the Belvedere of the
Continental Hilton,
Mexico, D.F.

Eres linda y hechicera
como una rosa

You are beautiful
and bewitching
like a rose
said the
high
hard
wire
in the elec-
tronic
phone
of the mike
which
led
from the
P.A.
to the loverly
head
of the
Intelligence
of the
cold ice
U.S.A.

the scent
of the clerk
at Merck
and
Merck
is the last
of the Devil's odor.

from the men's room wall
to the heart of all
        hello America
        said the television
    now hear this:

                                        In the Mansions of Cancer Gulch

        a man who
        smokes cigar
        is suckling
        stick which smells
        like it's just
        been stuck in

        bowls and bowls
        and bowls of
        commercials

recant dear sir
        said susskind
        seizing on his watch
        ends are open
        but beans are closed
        my doctor tells
        me Freud was quick
        to smoke cigar

oh, David, said the static
     we did a testimony
     on him like testimonial
     and still he died
     from
     gulch
     of the jaw,
       dig?

     Yes, said David
     but he bore
     the pain
     bravely

     some men
     are born
     to bore

Exodus

Goodbye America,
    Jesus said.
Come back, *boy!*
    we cried
    too late.

The Inaugural Ball

1.

There was a time
        when fornication
        was titanic
and the Devil
        had to work
        to cheat a womb.

                (pride of his teeth
                        on a root
                        long enough
                                to
                        pluck it out
                        the green wet sea
                        of the pussy slue
                        and down a falling
                                flight
                        of cellar stairs
                        hard, dark, deep
                        into the maiden brown
                        rooting out the bowels
                        which fell
                        like assassins
                                upon the white foam
                                of God's arrow)

2.

There was a time
    when fornication
    was satanic
and the Devil
    had to work
    to cheat a womb.
            (licked the liqueur
                of milady's loot
                off a hot feathered face
                and sobbed in despair
                as God won the race
                to shoot the fury
                of his intentions
                to the proper place.

3.

But now the devil
                smokes a cigar
                and has his nose
                up U.S. Phar-
                maceutical
The assassins
                who fall on God's
                white arrow
                give off the fumes
                of chemical
                killer bedded
                in vaseline
                as heroic
                in its odor
                as the exhaust
                which comes off a
                New York City
                Transportation
                System Bus.

4.

I do not want
     to believe it.
(Ay, no quiero verla!)
   that the scent
      of the clerk
      at Merck
         and
         Merck
      is the last
         of the Devil's odor.

No.
   I want
to declaim
that the time
   will return
   when
   Lucifer wrestles
   the Lord again
      for fucking
   all glory
   of heaven's vault
         in flame,
         and
         mandarins
         mad
         with
         fright
         at fucking
         and God's
         black
         light.

Timing

Listen
   my love
   the hour
   is late
   my side
   has an
   ache
     If
     you don't
     get a
     taxi
     my heart
     will break